Maybe You Never Loved Me As Much As You Loved New York

A Collection of Poems

By Rebecca Routh-Sample

Maybe You Never Loved Me As Much As You Loved New York

All rights reserved. This book or any portion thereof may not be produced in any manner without the express written permission of the author. Brief quotations are okay in review.

ISBN 9781445787770

Copyright 2024 by Rebecca Routh-Sample

Published 2024 by Lulu Press Inc

Maybe You Never Loved Me As Much As You Loved New York

Other books by Rebecca Routh-Sample

Fiction

Diary Of A Teenage Fangirl

Diary Of A Teenage Rebel Girl

Poetry

ghost world

donnie darko

paramour

Spinner's End

The Greatest Love Story Never Told

Maybe You Never Loved Me As Much As You Loved New York

If You're Reading This, I Have Some Questions

All available to purchase on www.lulu.com and www.Amazon.com

Maybe You Never Loved Me As Much As You Loved New York

Connect with me on social media if you want! I'd love to hear your feedback:

Twitter: @itsbeccafy

Instagram: @beccafyofficial

TikTok: @itsbeccafy

Check out Amy's artwork:

Instagram: @amyleylaart

And buy her prints on Etsy:

www.etsy.com/uk/shop/PetrichorCorner

Maybe You Never Loved Me As Much As You Loved New York

Contents

1. New York
2. My Last Chance At Love
3. On This Sunny Afternoon
4. Plastics
5. Bleach
6. Action
7. Burn The Witch
8. Doom
9. Shy Guy
10. Judas Escariat
11. Energy Vampire
12. I Found You
13. Be
14. Together
15. Best Intentions
16. Forever Friend
17. You're The Reason
18. Sometimes
19. Sirens
20. Take The Night
21. Closer
22. That's All I Really Know
23. You Can't Bring Back The Dead

Maybe You Never Loved Me As Much As You Loved New York
   24. Run Like Hell
   25. Minnows

Maybe You Never Loved Me As Much As You Loved New York
New York

I can see you dancing with
your sister father daughter
dance
Ever since you left town you
missed her and your mother
because she raised you all on
her own
so when you're up North
that's why you
wish you were back in New
York

We wandered round the graveyard
in the village near my house I cried
for my grandmother and the
others that I've lost
How I wish I could rewind time
Push up daisies myself but you pull
me to your body
and kissed every tear that fell

I need to be near my family of course but that's
why you wish you were back in New York

Perplexed because I
don't get what they
can't see, but I get
reminded every
time you're with me

Maybe You Never Loved Me As Much As You Loved New York
Sent from above to
save me
never once tried to change me

Maybe I knew you in another life

This is all I've ever wanted

All I can see is you

My Last Chance At Love

I should've taken the last train
I should've danced in the rain I
should've gone to see Black Widow
that weekday in July and at the Airbnb
I should've said
'Sorry, I've got a prior engagement'.
should've crossed the river ouse
straight to you and gone to the Slug
and Lettuce for drinks because time
fades quickly you have no chance to
blink shake the polaroid picture
only to let the past shrink into a
snapshot of something you don't
recognise anymore and you're cold
as a corpse covered in rose thorns
and people will pass by your grave
and a small child asks 'Who was
she?' when you thought the most

Maybe You Never Loved Me As Much As You Loved New York

frightening question was 'Who is
she?' or 'Who am I?' because you
answer 'I don't know' and the mother
answers to her child 'I don't know'

On This Sunny Afternoon

If you've ever felt sun-stained
like a fruit fly on a hot day
Burned out Coca Cola and
flat sizzling lemonade
Sandwiches with mayonnaise
basket full of food to taste but my
lips are cherry chapstick glossy
and saliva stained Taste me and I
promise you'll feel better
Keep me in an invisible locket
Because I'm your scarlet letter
I promise you ain't tasted nothing better
I promise you in 5 minutes you'll forget her It would take
seventy lifetimes to forget me but you've already got me
so soon
in this life
on this sunny afternoon

Maybe You Never Loved Me As Much As You Loved New York
Plastics

I wouldn't replace him for any damn thing in the world If you live with regrets its because you didn't live right and you didn't move right
and then you'll never be able to sleep at night and you'll blame everybody else in every single fight
and you'll find a plastic doll to fill your fantasies
and when you die
there's not a single real thing left of you

Leave creative
licence to the
creators and fighting
to the gladiators and
the love to the lovers
and romance to the
romantics and the
plastic to the plastics
leave the plastic
to the plastics

He's not just a footnote in the story of your life
He's a fully fledged character in his own damn right
He existed before you
and will exist after you
His mother birthed him
Not you

Own your bad
ideas He's not a
drug a numb-er a

Maybe You Never Loved Me As Much As You Loved New York
distraction or a
number

Bleach

Taken time
It tooketh time
Cinnamon candle
Bottle of wine

The loneliest night
The longest time
The striking hand
The biggest crime

Trapped in a cage of my own creation
Search for the worst destination
Obsession and hyper-fixation
Standing on the edge of that old
train   station Drinking blood
because i'm impatient   Alone in the
corridor like an inpatient I look in
my eyes but I can't see Dig I my nails
in but I don't feel a thing my mind
felt cluttered
but now i'm so empty

Bleached my personality
Ripped my life story to the seems
Burned my birth certificate and family tree

Maybe You Never Loved Me As Much As You Loved
New York
Dug myself a hole called
it a grave Buried alive for
sixty days
No one checked if i was okay They all
say 'she's gone away' but where
would I even stay? And what else
would they even say?

Action

Wailing like a banshee
she should date me why
can't she?

Ask her at first
Tease her second
Third I called
Fourth she beckoned
Fifth I reckoned
Sixth she changed her mind
Seventh I pulled a gun on her
Eighth she didn't cry

They locked me away
Put me in chains Boys will be boys
but everyone agreed
wholeheartedly
'It was your fault girl it was
your fault nobody would
have been

Maybe You Never Loved Me As Much As You Loved New York
threatened
if you'd just given it'

and it was also video games, music
and TV it was an
absent father and
explicit poetry

It was never me
The golden boy

My ivory protected me My
anatomy protected me We
burned her at the stake and
sentenced her to 50 years and
if the glove fits you won't equit
because it was only five minutes of action

It was just an action like
action refusing me is a
violent action

Burn The Witch

Diana the
plague is in
your hands
Pushed the wicked witch of the North
down the stairs so now you'll just be
damned

Maybe You Never Loved Me As Much As You Loved New York
We've all got our eyes on you and it isn't in our plan For cinderella go to the ball and outshine her man
We'll leave you in rags if you question the indiscretions of the Crown We'll cast you aside like a troll in our mentions and no one gives a damn about your intentions

We won't hesitate to burn the witch We won't hesitate to burn the witch

Doom

Battered, beaten and bruised
All used up by you
All the weight that I lose
A dream fading to black
Neglected massive attack
sharpened the knives to turn on my self when the razors blades dull

Maybe You Never Loved Me As Much As You Loved New York
Depths of despair
drowning simple
and clean muffled
howling straight at the
moon because the
lone wolf has
succumbed to
the loneliest doom

Scary being alone In the most crowded
room holding trophies made out of gold
that chips away the moment it dawns on
you're empty lonely Can you just hold me?
I can't see you in the dark you used to
shine so bright it was like sunshine and
sparks Magic man
in a blizzard of cold
touches burn like a
phoenix erodes
from the ashes
when you're done
and the bastards
have won oldest
story anybody ever
damn told

and the worlds doesn't end
but it turns without any
purpose at all there's nowhere
to fall trapped
no point to it all

Maybe You Never Loved Me As Much As You Loved New York
Shy Guy

I used to think you were a shy guy
But now I know that you are just a sly guy
I'm just gonna pop another pill and sleep just fine
I may be crazy but at least I'm not sly

Thought we were solid, but you're just a snake
It thought it was real, but now I know's all fake

So if we're not friends, are we enemies?
If we're not star-cross'd lovers, are we cursed deities? Are we born to die, or were you born just to lie?
Was I destined to fly too close to the sun and just... die?

You used me and abused me and threw me away Because I was old and boring and as not as bright and shiny

You're not a shy guy
You're not a nice guy

Judas Escariat

I dub thee Judas Escariat
That is a more fitting name
My name is L Lawliet
I'm ahead of your game
You will lead me to my death

Maybe You Never Loved Me As Much As You Loved New York
But you're not Jesus
And you're nobody's saviour
You disciples are easily swayed
The angels aren't in your favour
And you can follow John all you like but one day he'll betray you
They always do, they always do

Pull me close and let me go
Put me through the ringer and send me home
I don't trust people who paint their own faces
It means they're narcissistic
And if you weren't suck a love struck fool, I'd say you were sadistic

Judas Escariat, you will lead me to my death
But I will be resurrected
I will be brought back to life
And I will feel more alive than you have in your entire life
You may be living in the big city
But you'll always be his wife

They'll dub me a hero, and you a scared cow
And they'll lead you to the slaughter
It'll all be fine somehow

I've done some bad things in my life, caused many people many strife
But I'm on the side of justice
You can see it in my eyes

Maybe You Never Loved Me As Much As You Loved
New York
You're living the high life now
But you'll pay the final price
is digging your grave John the
Baptist is digging your grave
And he'll bury you in it
After he's driven you insane

Karma comes back around

Energy Vampire

Only a miserable person would
find optimism boring Only a hateful
person would make fun of you for
being excited about something and
if they drain you of every single
damn thing that makes you you
just let them get slew because you
only have one
life
so you better God damn do you

not everybody's gonna like you
and not everybody's gonna like it
but the only way you get rid of
an energy vampire is to run far,
far away from it

Some people are just miserable
they're in a right state but their

Maybe You Never Loved Me As Much As You Loved New York
bad day doesn't decide your
fate
No one can make you feel inferior
without your consent No one can
steal your light if you deflect
Nobody can chase you down down
if you defect Your zest for life is
not a defect

Meet me in the back room we'll
no-clip out of this place Take
my hand
We'll get away from this bad place
I love you
Let's run
Let's have some fun

I Found You

I found you deep in the centre
of the public swimming pool
ripping out your hair and
eyelashes All of your skin
tattoos and gashes blood
flowed in the water and I
jumped in to save you even
though I can't swim and you'd
do the same for me gave you
the kiss of life I think that's all you
need

Maybe You Never Loved Me As Much As You Loved New York

Be

My AirPods broke my life's a
joke my oldest love wants me
to choke no job I'm broke I'm
just waiting to meet a decent
bloke and I'm sure they just
want me to overdose nobody
has ever came close I'm just
a girl from Etsy with a
homemade tote and that
same hope I had when I was
fifteen When I believed
people couldn't do bad things
but every day I'm proven
wrong by the same old news
and the same old songs how
humanity sucks what if the
earth tilted and we all
dropped off Is this covid or a
really bad cough? Is this
abuse or is it just a job?
the world going to burn alive
from our own damn
greed

Maybe You Never Loved Me As Much As You Loved New York
I've stopped trying to tell the future
I'm going to be

Together

You deserve a girl that's Going bat for you bring you out on the red carpet say 'that's my man' for you Kiss while a million camera's flash Kiss you when you're the only two left on Earth or 7 billion we're meant to be

I'm not even trying to be mean
I just don't see what you see when the novelty runs out you'll be free heartbreak but you can piece it back together with me

let's build a life
TOGETHER
let's brave the stormy weather TOGETHER
let's run with the wolves together
TOGETHER
sting like a scorpion
TOGETHER
hit the bullseye, archer
TOGETHER

Maybe You Never Loved Me As Much As You Loved New York

Best Intensions

Every guy I date is an
overcorrection too much
neurosis to mention you are
the king of my heart
but it
was a rigged election
psychological itch justifying
the dramatic tension and I
go
around to everyone
sliding in their
mentions I
promise
you
I had the best intentions

Because You're The Reason

Slept in on Sunday counted
eyelashes 'til Monday caramel
frappucino dancing around the
movie's hero Benny and June
you looney tune in April, May
and summer rain you stepped
right of a poster I had when I
was fifteen when I watched
that movie on repeat wish i

Maybe You Never Loved Me As Much As You Loved
New York
knew who Charlie wrote those
letters to better ask Stephen
Chbosky How I love you how I
paint your brown eyes blue
don't know what you're running from
but I'm running straight to you wait for
me and your electricity He broke my
heart to smithereens but you stopped
the car crash before it maimed me
permanently and I never wanted a
simple life but I still never wanted this
but you make all of this worth it with
every single kiss
It's just bliss

and you're the reason

Sometimes

I used to love you always now I
love you most days then I
loved you some days now I
love you in some ways

Now I love you sometimes
or sometimes not at all
Sometimes I hate you
sometimes i just want to
bash your head against the
wall

Maybe You Never Loved Me As Much As You Loved New York

Sirens

If another angel shall fall
I promise you, I'll leave it all I'll
still be the queen of storms but i
won't be here to get soaked in
the rainstorm when it stops
being fun I'll leave you the same
way i left one true love   and yes
it was crazy and full of devotion
but sometimes love isn't
enough

jump into the sea and drown
with me but reach the surface
in time to hear the sirens sing
with the torment
they bring

Take The Night

Maybe
the days of shutting
down McClaren's are
gone

Maybe You Never Loved Me As Much As You Loved
New York
I still think I saw you at
the restaurant how'd we
end up here so soon?
sometimes I wish I knew
if I could go back in time

I was from staten island never
had a dad but I held on to
hope and I ran as fast as i can
to New York City and met a girl
she was from a different world
and I dated a lot of girls but
they weren't you If it was up
to me
I'd just go back in time

Let's take the night go
to a club take the night
run through Manhatten
take the night

because if it's not you
it's not gonna be anyone

because if it's not you
it's not gonna be anyone

Maybe You Never Loved Me As Much As You Loved New York

Closer

Why don't you just come closer?
I'll kiss you like a poster on my
bedroom wall
like I'm thirteen when
you still called

I thought these days would
last longer than they are but
it's becoming faster and
faster and even just as hard
you try to hold onto it
like a firefly in a jar I'd
like to make myself
believe that planet
earth turns slowly but
hours pass like
minutes and I'm just
as lonely

I wish you were closer like
I'm fifteen and you still
called

i wish you were closer i wish
i could bring you closer

i just miss you sometimes

Maybe You Never Loved Me As Much As You Loved New York

That's All I Really Know

I was so young and dumb I
thought I could do anything
thought I could catch an angel
with a pair of mechanical wings
I thought fairytales were fiction
I thought I'd overcome my life's greatest addiction

but I met you and you
floored   me
gave a new name to my
longing when I thought
I'd never
love again I saw you you
were there Saturday night
blonde hair my twin flame
my longest night my only
fight did we know each
other life I'm so blessed I
found you
this time

I never ever ever want to watch you go
that's all I really know

Maybe You Never Loved Me As Much As You Loved New York

You Can't Bring Back The Dead

You know fine well you don't pray for
somebody's balance because you
know you can't pray for a bank balance
houses and racks and a heart like a hole go
ahead try to fill it with gold carve a
new one from stone

you can't bring back the dead transmutation   the infinity
stone philosopher's stone Phoenix down rock n roll
tribute concert funeral hologram god damn black magic
hex
drugs money
yet
but you can't bring back the dead you
can't bring back the dead

Run Like Hell

It ain't worth having a baby nowadays
Men are unreliable
Obsessed with a dream, it's undeniable
I'm not a doll, I can't be everything
Nor do I want to be

Don't become a baby mama

Maybe You Never Loved Me As Much As You Loved New York
To man made out of trash
Don't take money from a man
That only has cash
Don't rely on anybody but yourself
Because one of these days you'll be chained down
And wanna run like hell

When you have the world at your feet
Talents and a tonne of dreams Why risk it all?
With a short fix to your insecurity
Work on it, don't ever settle
For a man with words so warm but a heart made of metal
And no respect for your struggle
It ain't worth it babe

Run like hell
From all those people telling you 'NO'
Even when your self worth is low
Tell em where to go
Don't sell your soul, your body, your words or your truth
Don't change your lips or worry whose proud of you
And don't you ever think you need anyone to complete you
'Cause that ain't true

The moral of the story
From a girl who almost lost it all
Is that you have to stand tall
Keep pushing forward because there are no perfect storms
Only happy endings

Maybe You Never Loved Me As Much As You Loved
New York
And if he ain't giving you 'em
Stop pretending.

Minnows

I used to laugh I used to
dream I used to catch
minnows and say funny
things run until my
knees went weak and sing so loud
until I fell asleep

I didn't need anything it
was just you and me if I
ever lost you I don't
know what I'd do

One day I'll lose you
And when I do I
don't know what I'll
do

Maybe You Never Loved Me As Much As You Loved New York

All rights reserved. This book or any portion thereof may not be produced in any manner without the express written permission of the author. Brief quotations are okay in review.

ISBN 9781445787770

Copyright 2024 by Rebecca Routh-Sample

Published 2024 by Lulu Press Inc

Maybe You Never Loved Me As Much As You Loved New York

Connect with me on social media if you want! I'd love to hear your feedback:

Twitter: @itsbeccafy

Instagram: @beccafyofficial

TikTok: @itsbeccafy

Check out Amy's artwork:

Instagram: @amyleylaart

And buy her prints on Etsy:

www.etsy.com/uk/shop/PetrichorCorner

Maybe You Never Loved Me As Much As You Loved
New York

Maybe You Never Loved Me As Much As You Loved
New York